How Much the Body

How Much the Body

Poems about Faith

LINDA LEE McDONALD

WIPF *&* STOCK · Eugene, Oregon

HOW MUCH THE BODY
Poems about Faith

Wipf & Stock
An Imprint of Wipf and Stock Publishers
199 W. 8th Ave., Suite 3
Eugene, OR 97401

www.wipfandstock.com

PAPERBACK ISBN: 978-1-5326-8450-0
HARDCOVER ISBN: 978-1-5326-8451-7
EBOOK ISBN: 978-1-5326-8452-4

Manufactured in the U.S.A.   07/11/19

To my children

(in order of appearance):

Clarence

Cordelia

Mitchell

Brittany

From the instructions that I received with the purchase
of a small personal humidifier:

Long hold the button to open the light

Contents

III. Suddenly, Robins

Acknowledgements

I would like to thank the AIR Serenbe artists-in-residency program and its director, Michael Bettis, for providing the space and time for me to write. While I did not craft this manuscript during my residency, AIR Serenbe allowed me to reclaim the writing voice that speaks throughout my work.

The following are people who have been indispensable to me in my evolution as a writer and a person: Cristin O'Keefe Aptowicz and her unwavering confidence in me; my graduate school teachers and crowd that taught me that craft that lies as a heartbeat beneath the art: Buddy Nordan, Chuck Kinder, Jan Beatty, Roger LePage, Michael Gerhard Martin, Dave Newman, Jane Herring, Micki Myers, Keely Bowers; the students who led me to articulate what I knew and then claimed it for their own: Stephanie Feldman, Caldwell Holden, Colleen Mayo, Naomi Shimada, Ciara LaVelle, Jessica Bylander, Micah Hauser, and many others; my lifelong friends who are my brains and my breath: Maude Myers, Margaret Mitro, Jill Wertz, Mandi Wright, Carolyn Hile, Anne Griffith, Jennifer Easterday, Paula Tyler, Ben Gross, Sue Burton and Sue Bridgers, Larissa Wolowec; finally, my pastors, bless their patient hearts: Reverend Homer Green and Pastor Gary Paladin.

And I would like to thank my family: you have always been there; you haven't always had to be, but there you are.

I.

Count, Tell, Say, Speak

My Feet at the Edge of the Swamp

What looks like death is only duckweed
and what feels like forever is a season—end
of summer, early spring, eternity arrives

in tiny pieces. At first, quiet; then an explosion
of cicadas. A bird, the song of frogs, above
and amid the humid, green muck.
The sun ascends to my left

and I wonder about the trees,

white and hollow
rootless ghosts, pushed by some tide
away from the wet

and soft earth. Eventually,
like all dead things, they fall. Because what is
created is also changed
by wind, or hunger, or gravity, or time.

In the distance, a woodpecker mimics time's
steady tocks. In a further distance, a rushing stream
of human traffic. At the edge of the holy origin

of all things,
I turn to look back.

Origin of Life

I. Bubbles

Here's one theory, paraphrased, from Joseph Panno: seashore,
hot sun. Waves whisk in, whisk out against rock
and dirt. From the broken stars came rock
and dirt. From the broken stars came air and the air
squeezed out water like silent weeping.

Before time, before being, before life—before one cell
multiplies into two, multiplies into forsythia and avocado
and dinosaurs, bears, ballet dancers, and district attorneys—

a layer of bubbles—*a delicate foam*—emerges
from the sea and the shore and the air and the heat and
the motion that began when the stars burst open. The bubbles
are the children of all of this. Eventually, from the rock,
oil seeps. Oil merges with the bubbles so the foam no longer
splits and forms anew—rather, the bubbles collide
within the rhythm that the water has established. Water
that has grown to be a sea.

The rhythm of the sea comes from gravity.
But not gravity from the pull of the moon. Probably
a moon has not yet been birthed with violence
from the belly of the earth and flung from the light
into half darkness. Sun evaporates water.
Bubbles gasp. One bubble joins
a protein to the water, splits without
separating, then grows.

Human babies sometimes begin as bubbles
in a glass of champagne. We split
without separating and we grow.

II. Strings

Physicists like Wolfgang Pauli dream of strings, the theory that explains
every single thing like quantum gravity, electromagnetism, why fathers
leave without dying, why mothers tell dreams about building blocks
of matter no one can see, dreams that physicists dream
of energy moving in strings, strings that wrap
dimensions large and small into tidy packages and
strings that resonate like a cello. No one has ever heard
this frequency. No one has ever seen such a string.
The universe unrolling like a ball of yarn will never wind up
smaller than the size of a string,
the string theorists promise. But when it does, if
it does become that small,

                                            they also promise

the universe will expand again.

III. Jellyfish

in the dark murky salt when the moon
begins its pull.
the placenta is a jellyfish.

between my legs, a doctor, fishing,
tugs her line and waits
while the baby is washed, weighed,
wrapped, dangled from the hook
of my breast. The new baby is an *always*,
is a *was meant to be.*

the doctor waits for the fish
she will not quite throw back.
it will come when it does

no struggle, no bearing down,
cramp of moon behind a cloud,
jellyfish rocking,

rocking towards the shore.

IV. Logos

Count, tell, say, speak
the uttered word and the word
remaining within:
I am;
let there be.

My First Christmas

Winter in Austin feels like spring anywhere else
so it felt like spring, and beginning again, outside
and inside of me. The first Christmas

I lived for God when I was alone
but was never alone.

Living for God was one of the ways to explain
what had happened. So was born again. It felt
like stepping from one life to another, from one room
to the same room in a new house.

Then my roommate, Anne, moved out of our apartment and
I lost my job as a waitress because I was differently different
now, obnoxious—they said—with religiosity, making everyone
uncomfortable with this incessant talk of God.
I only knew that soon

after the holidays
after something
my new life
would begin
for real.

Of course, per usual, I had no money.

I took my dog on thousands of walks along a woodsy trail
and I worried about what would happen
to him once I was raptured. I prayed
that my dog would instantly, painlessly, die
the moment my feet left the ground
because I imagined how sad he would be, barking
at the shape of me dwindling like a balloon
released into the sky. I wept and prayed for him,
for all sweet, unredeemable dogs.
I found a tree on one of these walks, a tree

that someone had thrown out
that was actually a cedar bush
and I dragged it into my apartment
to decorate with the few decorative things
I owned: popcorn on thread and thin metal
ornaments of the Twelve Days of Christmas,
the song of which I sang to myself in the loud
quiet of my singular voice in the apartment
newly emptied of everything
that had been Anne's. My apartment smelled
like Christmas but my allergies went crazy.
Austin, Texas. Cedar fever.

That year, every member of my family
sent me a crèche for a Christmas. Jesus and Mary
and Joseph, crafted from pebbles, glass, porcelain,
carved out of wood, some with wise men, some
with sheep and a cow. This included a big headed
Precious Moments nativity snow globe
and Santa alone, kneeling to the baby.

It was difficult to talk to my family back then, even long distance.
They were suspicious that I would say something about religion that failed
to show them in a positive light. And they were right.
All I knew then was what I had been told and what I felt
but what I barely understood. I repeated phrases
and scripture without wisdom or patience.
The Bible said I had power to be a witness.
But not to my folks, not over the phone.

I called an old boyfriend and tried to save him.
We argued as passionately as ever—but about better things
]than we had argued about before.
I have the one true religion! I shouted.
I have the one true religion! he shouted.
And I tried to save my friend—my best friend from second grade.
Religion is personal, she told me.
I made out with your boyfriend

the summer after sophomore year. I told her, angry.
That's personal. I bet you want to hear about that.

I repented of both conversations. But not of wanting
to save people.

There was not enough church to give me plenty to do.
Some nights, I drank coffee at Sister Carolyn's
until I shook for hours, then woke up shaking
from caffeine and revelation.

Next door the Christmas party I had previously attended
was full on with weed and beer and stoned women
lugging out pans of holiday food so proud
of their grandma's cast iron recipes.
This year, I was invited but not really invited.

The first Christmas that I lived for God, I went shopping
for dog food and peanut M&Ms at the grocery store
where I used to buy beer. And the music that always plays
at Christmas that no one listens to sang out God and sinner
reconciled. Which is what had happened to me, so recently,
that I started to cry, right there, in the dog food aisle.

Because when He found me, my life was like a terrible story
I once read in the newspaper where a girl, blind and deaf,
accidentally fell to her death from a four story building.
My life had been like that—falling and falling
and falling, waiting to hit, waiting to die, afraid to die,
not wanting to die, not wanting to fall, only I fell

only I fell into a Christmas card
full of angels and shepherds
and donkeys and wise men and camels
and Jesus.

It was like that. My first Christmas. It was exactly like that.

Creation Story and the Fall of Man

This one begins with a cow or maybe ten cows or a dairy farm full
of cows but definitely with a stainless steel industrial-sized butter churn
and a refrigerator the size of a department store window with shelves
that can be reorganized into a variety of options for space and size.

This creation story is a metaphor, interpreted through a butter sculpture
carved into a bust of Will Rogers for the Iowa State Fair.

In this metaphor, the butter sculpture becomes a type
of Adam (once famous as part of the duo, Adam and Eve)
where the sculptor is God; this metaphor also works
for any primordial man emerging through the concept of fate
or a science based, secular humanist, universally accepted
version of evolutionary theory. So imagine, you, the reader,
each choosing his own God or notgod; imagine, further, your chosen
creative force choosing butter to construct
the human masterpiece. Michelangelo chose marble. God
chose dirt and spit. This one, butter.

In the beginning, the chisel glides like homilies
until it crafts the face of a man who never met a man
he didn't like, malleable as a saint on the front pew.
And the crowds of fairgoers and farmers (who represent
the interpreters of said metaphor) are old enough or savvy
enough to be amazed: Will Rogers! How life like
the bust and how the smell of butter resurrects sepia memories
of old fashioned movie theaters and baking from scratch;
buttery crust, buttered dinner rolls, babies and puppies and the time he stole
and ate an entire stick of butter in its plain, perfect, salty,
sweet, greasy goodness. Will Rogers, butter sculpture, Iowa State Fair.
Blue Ribbon winner.

Imagine further in the way that metaphor requires further
imagining. This Adam does not need hot sin
and his woman's fast talking snake to lose his footing -
it only has to be five, ten degrees warmer than it is inside your fridge

at home. Enter the creature's heart now, and feel the shock,
the surprise when his bland, mild face registers
his end, understanding that—prepared or unprepared
for what comes next—his God has found him. Of course,
like all men when the details finally reveal themselves, the clarity
of Will Rogers' oleaginous eyes churn. A shift
occurs in the contours of his face. Laugh lines dig
more deeply, plow furrows down his cheeks, trenches
for tears. The world grows heavier and heavier.
And thus begins his slick descent.

That Time the Father of Faith Pretended His Wife Was His Sister

Abraham had faith to pack up all of the things
he had purchased or made in Ur to follow
his newly discovered Lord into anywhere.

He had faith to serve dates
and fatted lamb to Melchizedek and to invent
paying tithes, to offer thanksgiving, and to circumcise

himself and all of the men in his household.
The promise as clear as the Milky Way
tumbling around the radiant moon

was obscured by sandstorms kicked up
by the face of a wife so beautiful
that Pharaoh stopped his chariots, just to look.

A look that could kill. And without his life
there would be no promise. No son, no
nations: it was too hard to know

that the name of the God of the Living meant
exactly that. It was too hard to see that beautiful,
compliant Sarai (who carried in her pocket

the kind of shame and jealousy that comes
with disappointing your man) also carried the singular
egg—tucked back and away from the cycles and rhythms

that emptied her into a shell month after month, after year,
after decade—the partner to Abraham's starry
seed. My sister, he called her, frightened into lying

on at least three occasions. And she, still beautiful,
even at ninety, waited in Pharaoh's harem for the next
heartbreak to touch her inner heart. Kept her mouth shut.

Oh she earned her not-so-secret belly laugh.
and the title of princess thrown in for good measure.
Abraham earned a trip up the mountain

with its panoramic view of the extinction of his name;
trudging as all brave and frightened souls trudge:
through the litter of his failings.

His faith grew in the way my own grew, in the little clouds kicked up
by dusty, tired feet, until finally, finally, his faith was able
to summon the angel that stayed his knife hand.

So the promise was kept, in its surprising way. And the lesson might not
    always be
the one we so often hear: that we are called upon
to identify and then claim a willingness to sacrifice what we love most

(one eye peeking from beneath these fervent, theoretical promises
in hope, in hope, that what we love most won't kill us in losing it)
and then struggle through the hope that shames us:

not this, please, I will love You anyway, but, please, not this.
Maybe the lesson is that the God of the Living will plant
tiny seeds for us to parent into and through our unknown lands

until they become magnificent trees we barely recognize
that shade and shelter whole flocks of birds; some memory of these seeds,
these trees, might throw a shadow to outlive our own certain deaths.

Maybe the lesson is that the God who held faith in Abraham
's faith—hidden as it was, sometimes, like a ram
in the brambles—holds the same faith in us.

Glory

It is true
that the Lord's glory
descends from heaven
like photos of sunlight
streaming through
darkness; some bear
witness to having seen
the shimmering
Shekinah cloud
hover above the saints.
It is equally true
that a single hand raised
up against the gravity
of this universe
to praise His name
is also His glory.

The Conductivity of Human Beings

They say lightning travels from the ground
to the sky and not from the sky to the ground
as it seems from a distance, from the ground;
this is how You travel within me, moving, within
to without, down to up: I am split by a jagged streak
until words splinter in my mouth.
I have felt lightening in someone else's hand
transfer to meet what has risen out of the earth

I am made of:
a cloud as it opens to rain
inside bones, inside
marrow and sinew,
rainbow and thunder, all at once,
light breaking through my heart
of prisomed glass—
that beautiful, that bright.

Fold

(Associated Press, 2005) Hundreds of sheep followed their leader off a cliff in eastern Turkey. Four hundred sheep fell fifteen yards to their deaths into a ravine but broke the fall of another 1,100 animals who survived.

I gave my footsteps to the sure feet to the fleet one
now before me and those feet gave their hoof beat
to the neat feet past the sheepgate where the sun heat
makes the grass sweet and the tail wag and the ram bleat.

Hooved feet follow ram bleat and hooved feet
follow clover toward the prophet of the shepherd crook
and His rod and His pen. Like seasons equinoctial
like the lambing and the shearing like the dog bark
and the quick bite the Shepherd calls our names.

First the hoof steps onto deep grass then the hoof steps
on the rocky path then the hoof steps onto nothing
and scramble and fall. Fall like quiet hoof-steps into
deep grass amid the buzzing of the green air with its hop
toads and its crickets and moles. We have lived here
borne our young here with our salt musk in the long grass.
We have learned what the earth is how the thin air
lines the deep gulf of the stone void full of danger,
where we fold upon fold upon fold upon fold.

Winter in the Goldfish Bowl

Dexter is dead.

The net descends on the slight frown
of Dexter's body. Once he had been all glint
and sparkle, a dancer in Vegas with plenty of money
and time to kill in the dressing room
with Zippy, his partner on stage and off.

Now Zippy's mouth pulses quick against the glass
like the heartbeat of a fetus. Below him
The filter churns and the rocks cast a hard pink
toward the empty grey castle.

Zippy swallows something, some floating speck, and he
circles once. He circles again, and then again.
A day of circles. A week. A year.

He still has the green plastic plant—a fern—
And his faint reflection to nudge and ponder.
An air bubble bursts as it touches the thin skin
between water and low hanging sky.

Circle the castle, taste the stones, the pulse of mouth and gill.

What so easily slips through my grasp are the few things
Zippy knows for sure:
the swish, the release and the rising.

Prayer of the Hem

too low for the hand
too slow for the foot
I reach for the hem
of the garment only
to be lifted to the Face

Tongues

I couldn't hear myself the first time
when there was too much noise and too many
other voices more insistent than mine.

But I felt? Goodness as a physical
thing, maybe. Brilliance
and love, personified.

When I heard myself, weeks later, alone
in my room, it was like so many other firsts
of mine: it sounded fake and not fake. It was me
and not me. Words and not words but prayer—
like looking into a pattern of dots or paisley swirls
that turn into dolphins or the Eiffel Tower
and you don't know at what point your eyes crossed
to make this happen. I don't know at which point
my tongue crossed to make this happen.

Tongues are said sometimes be a real language
that someone might know. Mine is definitely not one
of the Khoisan Click languages or Mongolian
throat singing—neither the tweedle of birds and mountain
streams nor the galloping horse variety. After years
of tongue speaking, my God words spill out butterflies
 and garter snakes and small fish and the music
of brass instruments in syllabic repetitions. But always
the tone is urgent and passionate, jittering and weeping
out more than I know how to say.

II.

An Infinite You, Somehow Surprised

The Woman Who Believes Every Prayer (Should Be Answered How She Likes)

Here is your radio alarm clock going off on time
despite last night's storm with what just happens
to be your favorite song. Here is your cloudless
morning, sunny, moderate temperatures exactly
when you need sunny, moderate temperatures. Here
are your favorite pair of jeans, clean, and they fit perfectly
because today has turned out to be a skinny tummy day.
Here is the blouse—and look!—that stain on the collar
has come out beautifully as has your perfect hair. Here is
your egg timer set for time with God and the Bible
that is also a coloring book. Here are your car keys;
they had fallen behind the dresser but you fortuitously
noticed a glint of metal as you brushed the perfect shade
onto your cheeks. Look at this! Plenty of gas in the tank
when you thought you had much less. And, by the way,
wonderful mileage for a car you purchased at a steal
in your favorite color. Your prayers are specific to color
and make and model because your God is a God of specificity;
your answered prayers are orders, perfectly filled. You give
credit to God. You give glory to God for His goodness
in all things. You are in His grace. Acknowledging
divine protection from the man in the Cadillac ahead
who fails to use his turn signal and when your green light
bursts greenly upon you—your lots of green lights in a row,
with very little traffic—here is your last-second swerve away
from that pothole. Here is your favorite parking space,
empty just for you. And after you are delighted to see
that your groceries are on sale, here is the manager
who happens by to provide your revenge on the cashier
who incorrectly reckoned your change.

Cordelia, Bowling

She likes the red ball best.
She waddles to the line, tumbles
the ball to the floor. She squats and
gives it a shove. The ball wanders
towards the pins. But here

is the loveliest thing. After she shoves the ball,
she flings her arms up over her head and she turns
and she dances and she never looks back to see
if she's knocked anything down.

She is tall for six years old.
Her eyes are brown and green.
There are two freckles on her left ear.
Beautiful is nothing compared to her.

Listen to what mothers learn from their daughters.
They learn *oh, that was me*; they learn *I could have
been her.* They learn a shortcut back
to their second birth—the joyful path through ordinary days:
every ball, every frame. Two games in a row.
Dancing. No looking back.

Tell me you won't forget whose daughter you are
and the liberty a daughter has to *just be.* Tell me,
daughter, that you will love yourself
this much for the rest of your life.

Close your eyes and feel

an expansion of self—you are sky bleeding
an infinite you, somehow surprised
to see how small, how eclipsed you become
at the edge of an ocean or mountain,
so large and so tiny all at once. Close
your eyes to understand that, inside skin,
you can be eternal and infinite.
This is how you might begin to embrace
that you came from God and will return to Him—
closing your eyes. This is also how you
might conceptualize there is no God,
or how to become your own God, yourself.
You are boundless possibility, and free will.

Hope that Stockpiles for Winter

Here is the metaphor: three children on a dairy farm
in western Ohio in 1965 or 66, in February,
chores to be done before the school bus comes.

Before them, a chill impossible to measure and only
a slit of sun on the horizon. Behind them, a kitchen
wallpapered with yellow roses.

Mother with blue eyes. Something warm on the stove—
oatmeal or Cream of Wheat. To move out into the cold,
the children cinch up, wince, cinch up, lead with the shoulder.
The snow is dry and light. They hide in their mufflers

from the wind but the wind still makes them cry.
The border collie that escorts them to the milk house
is not for playing with. To water the cows is to balance

between two buckets, arms never long enough
to keep the sloshing away from the pants,
which will freeze on the way back to the house.

To feed the calves is to dig so deeply into a barrel of feed
that both feet rise up off of the ground.
With the first kick, the scoop reaches the bottom.

The last kick pushes you back out. In a patch of leafless trees
at the corner of the far sixty acres, one abandoned nest
is wedged between two branches. Wind blows across the snow

like it blows across sand, into ridges and shadows. Here is where
the children learn the beauty of the strictest and coldest kind
of hope. The kind that exacts work—nothing given for nothing.

The kind of hope that stipulates order, discipline—to leave the warm bed,
make up the warm bed, leave the house, work, is the ritual of faith.
This is hope that stockpiles for winter, for the end of things.
Hope that after loss, there will be work to do that will still matter,

that after God takes away that last cloudy breath, He will return
to scoop up grief like a mitten full of flimsy snow and He will
toss it away—pieces of it scattering, landing with the softest sound.

Stand at the Door and Knock

It's as simple as being ten years old astride the stout bough
of an ancient tree in spring—that close to life, that safe, high
above the ground. It's like two people on either side
of a door, touching the door, leaning into, against

the door. The door absorbs the rhythm
of breathing. It creaks to that rhythm. The wood itself
breathes. A hand on one side brings up a hand to the other. Lips
on one side bring lips to the other.

Until there is no door. Just breathing. In and out. Two, one.
Hand rising to meet hand. I have no defender. You
are my defender. In and out. Two, one. I am all alone.
You are not alone. I am with you always. One

of us is a Shulamite.

But we are only ten years old—the place where I fall
backwards into memory, forward into dread. Breathing in
and out my rattles and my reeks. I can be taken to the doorway
but stepping through requires my own clumsy feet: the sweetness

of this knowing is a miracle

that echoes into the intimacy of salvation: I am with you
always. What upsweep of gratitude can I heave into His
branches, but myself, this damaged lucky self? His hand reaches
into the beehives and the stingers interspersed between the nests
of songbirds and hollows full of owls. I hear songs of golden coins

falling from the sky, falling falling: golden coins like feathers, like
 identical snowflakes. Who could believe in it? I do. Faithless
servant that I have been, would I choose miracles over money?

Would I shift back beneath the weight
of familiar burdens rather than face the tedious climb
of unhurriedly answered prayers? The shadow of the now
stretches beyond what little I have seen

of eternity. Heave me up into the sunlight, Lord; deliver
me from my own slow crawl, from the cluttered awakening
of my faith-leap into life.

Beautiful, Beloved

Beautiful, beloved, when I first met you,
my back was wedged against a closet door
trying to keep the monsters inside
and in my hand, for luck, was a penny.

I thought it might a dollar or a five
or a thousand dollars
or all of the dollars
I would even need
 in my whole expensive life. But
it was really just
a corroded green penny.

Beautiful, beloved, in a move I did not see coming
you slew the biggest monster
in my closet and then instructed me
in killing: hold *this* one by the neck, hold
that one by the tentacles. You made me kill
the ones I had tried to tame into pets.

Then you asked me for the penny—no,
you pried it from my hand. And replaced it
with gifts: an emerald tree frog
mist curling the base of a hill
moonlight
the shocking leap
of a gazelle
a sprig of lilac, the bright
moment light shines
through water.

Beautiful, beloved, my revelation
is this: I am no longer here
for miracles or power
or epiphanies from angels
or even for an entrance

into the golden eternity you built
with your own hands. I am here for this reason:

when loneliness echoed inside of me
like a copper coin dropped
down a deep well, metallic tick tick
ticking against stone walls—

such a long way down
like breath held too long,
like water unexpectedly deep,
or the way grief mimics depression mimics
anger; when I didn't see how the mouth
of this well was the jagged maw of a beast—

You caught what there was left to catch
and from these fragments, created some other
me, the same me, one less covetous
of my own wounds.

Beautiful, beloved,
I love You because you make me trust
the shimmering fish skin of faith.
I love You because You make me feel
like the girl I never was, never thought I could be.
You make me feel like some beautiful, happy girl
sitting on a porch swing on a purple summer evening
and You are my sweet first kiss.

Slow Danger

We dream about the blindsiding, the car accident
or the stranger chasing us faster than our thumping
hearts: the sudden, the unexpected, so immediate
the danger has no name. But we should have
been taking care of that old electrical wiring
in the attic; we shouldn't have eaten
that last double-bacon cheeseburger.
We have been warned, many times, to be warier
of the arthritic tiger in its cage; we should have
noticed how large the anaconda had grown—first
a number two pencil, now a glistening yellow tree
trunk, he eases like an ancient pit of tar
around the neck of the one who fed him
all of those baby mice by hand for all of those years.
We should have been more careful when we crossed
the street they were paving because we slipped
onto the path of the heavy roller inching along like indifference.

Like indifference, the opposite of love and of love's cousin,
hate; indifference, with its lukewarm seduction
of complacency, apathy. The road sign, like all signs,
might be from God; it reads *Slow Danger*. Far out to sea,
a storm stirs itself into a tropical depression,
its lackadaisical winds propel fat clouds full of our tears.

What Can Be Shaken

Be brave enough to pray for the shuffle.
And then the shake. For the heathen
to become righteous and for the pointing finger
to confound you, leave you frightened
at the sound of acorns tumbling and branches
sweeping across your roof.

Pray for something larger than you can
comfortably contain, the unremitting, the inevitable
encroaching thunder. At the first sound of it, count
to ten and divide by three—hope that the arrival
of lightning can be calculated. Intuiting that the mystery
of what might be revealed can be frightening

in its imprecision. We can share the grace of fear—
each of us alone in our private nights. The mercy
of individually crafted evolution careens into strange
directions, shakes us from pedestals upon which
we have placed our fallible selves.

Sliding Back: Eaten by Birds, Choking on Thorns

1. Amber

It was not a car accident
or a branch snapping beneath my feet
but the way a mosquito must have felt
alighting on a damp piece of goo
that catches and holds and hardens
into amber, the mosquito decorates
the hollow of a beautiful throat
protected by sensors in a museum exhibit
a jewel among jewels, so lifelike.
The artifact of a tiny life. So lifelike
that for a million years no one knew
how quickly it had smothered.

2. Oil and Virgins

At first, no one could tell.
Like baby not old enough to speak
appears wiser than she is,
my thoughts were not seen
on the outside of my face.
Inside, I turned so slowly
like a bored wife
from my prayers,
night after night hoping
He didn't want anything
but my shoulder, hoping
He didn't notice me. Finally they saw:
love Him, just love Him they told me
but I had already fallen asleep.

3. Hermit Crab in the Sydney Opera House

Do not underestimate my strength of will.
as I move from shell to shell,
as I press my form against each new wall
each new wall slick as a polished fingernail.
I am the snapper of clever claws.
I am the unfastener of the sensual mouth.
I am the most beautiful of all crabs
and I reproduce at will.
Such an appetite, such an appetite.
I will grow to fill up a taxi cab,
a city bus, a concert hall.

4. Prodigal

When I embarrass you
tell yourself it was the glittering lights
it was the drugs and sex
the billboard advertisement of the kitty cat
woman lapping from a giant bottle
purring beside the exit lane of a highway.
Tell yourself it was the curriculum
in the public school health class
that demonstrated the banana and the condom.

I know it was my mother's love
for food, her dissatisfaction kneaded
into bread, bubbled under cheese.
She is so fat, I'm afraid it's going to kill her.
Unless my father kills her first.
Unless his anger kills him first.
His love of anger.

It was their willingness to be so strange.
It was their unwillingness to be honest.
It was the way they protected me
from my own childhood. It was living

so near to and so far from what was promised,
what You promised. How everything is possible,
and how everything is supposed to be a certain way.
Nothing ever was.

5. Not Everyone Wants to Be a Soldier

How angry I can still become
with someone, something I battled years ago.

War is tedious. I want something
ordinary. Who could blame me for wanting

something ordinary? I let go
of my own balloon

to become less of a pilgrim. Don't you see?
almost none of the people who live in the city

where I have found myself
are even from there.

6. Image

I
tried
to
fit
but
the
box
felt
too
small
too
narrow
too
shallow

for
even
one
of
my
feet.

Latch

1.
This is a true story and also a parable, real and true, both.

When you are the smallest and the lightest, it is always your job
to be lifted to the sill of the kitchen window or to crawl through
a squat basement aperture to open the door for everyone else.
It is always dark. The arms that lift you wobble. There is a spider
web to creep through, but never a choice. You must.
There is no other way in. There is no one else who can.
Especially true in the days before cell phones quadruple bound us
into each other's business, when there was less quick rescue and more
more upstretched wobbling arms.

My locked door story takes place on a Wednesday night
in February, 1989, days before an ice storm glazed Austin, Texas.
I was not the smallest or the lightest of any crowd, three days
away from giving birth to my first child. A boy, I said,
in the way that mothers sometimes say with conviction,
but without proof. I'm not sure now how sure I felt about knowing
it would be a boy. What I remember was not knowing
how to birth or what it would be like or what it would be like after that.

2.
Everything was always my fault but nothing was never to my credit.

The husband I married so soon after my conversion was working hard
to shape me into something other than me. He believed
in a woman's duty to be submissive in ways I could not guess at. His Bible
backed him up. He offered as evidence of his goodness that he never hit
     me
with a closed fist. He accused me of bruising too easily. But we were
doing ok that day or that moment, maybe. I was doing, I thought,
while no longer really able to think, the right thing—being a wife, having
babies.

After church that Wednesday night, we went right home
instead of going out to Chili's or Jim's Restaurant with the church
friends who knew our problems and who prayed for us. A few of them
let me run to their houses if I had to. For reasons I no longer remember,
our front door was locked. And for other reasons
I no longer remember, we did not have a key to our own door.
Everyone we had given a spare key to was out. Inside,
 the dog barked to let us know that we should come in.
A metal rod was stationed in the gully of our sliding glass back door
because the neighborhood had burglars. It began to rain.

My husband ran to the back to check to see if he could somehow
jiggle that metal rod out of its gully. He didn't want to
have to break a window. I was nine months pregnant and the missing key
was going to be my fault.

Jesus, I prayed, *You could open this door* and the words made me laugh
because of course, of course He could, even if He didn't.

I reached to turn the handle. I decided to just turn it, not add any fancy
maneuvers. I turned the handle, the doorknob lock twisted
like someone on the other side of the door had opened it.
I went inside and then let my husband in through the back door.

3.
He did not quite believe in a miracle affiliated with me but there
it was.

His face was a little envious. He checked the doorknob
a few times. But I knew what this tiny miracle meant, maybe only
to me: that the Lord had His hand on this birth and, I thought,
on some of the other things that were on its way and I worshipped Him
and the next day I told everyone I could think to tell
about the way the knob twisted, like someone was there.

When the ice storm came a day or so later, my husband laughed
about how fat I was and how no one could lift me if I slipped on the ice
and fell. How he could have to call the fire department for a winch
hooked up to the biggest truck. Another day after that and there was the
   boy.

4.
Oh young and pregnant me who knew so little but felt so much,
this is for you.

Ahead of you, throughout the years of healing ahead, rivers
and oceans of rain will fall and you will sometimes have only
broken umbrellas blown inside out by a gust of wind.
Closed fists will not be the only weapon to bruise you; in fact,
closed fists will sometimes be mercifully recognizable as weapons
while the others will be disguised. Many handles will be unmovable,
will not flinch despite how urgently you will reach for faith
through shards of broken window glass. Your arms will wobble
out of fear and desperation and exhaustion as you lift up
your smallest ones into what appears to be darkness and
cobwebs.

But oh young and pregnant me, you lost count
years ago—believe this one true thing—you lost count
of how many times a lock was miraculously undone
from the other side. You've lost count of the joy
that came with each opening, every time.
Just in time. Just for you.

III.

Suddenly, Robins

Example of How God's Timing Is Often a Surprise

Winter, winter, winter, winter, winter, winter,
winter, winter, winter, winter, winter, winter,
winter, winter, winter, winter, winter. Suddenly
robins.

Strawberry Picking

Our eyes so recently safe do not easily recognize
this color—red—so we first reach towards something
pale. Then it appears, the tip of a wounded thumb,
the color of birth, maybe miracle, maybe joy.

We walk sandy paths plucking beads
you could buy Manhattan with.
My boy wrestles leaf and stem, feeds himself
fist by fist. He reveals his strategy:
If there's a juicy one that gets torn? I eat it.
As he bends I see his boxer shorts
And the small of his back: in him lives every boy
who ever chunked rocks into a pond.

My girl describes the shapes of berries
and clouds. She sees herself as far ahead
of her brother. *We both are*, she says,
generously aligning herself with my half empty pail.
We're winning, she says.
Then she brings a strawberry to her mouth—
a strawberry the size of a child's heart.
Wind picks at the hair beside her face
as she gazes at the sweetness inside of her. Five bites
before she licks her fingers and I recognize
this moment as a gift from the Lord.

Babies evaporate while their parents are trying
to get some sleep.Even now I forget how large
the eyes, how sweet the whorl at the top of the head,
the way a finger crooks into a perfect mouth,
the sound of the hiccup after the crying has stopped.
Once I was called to be their whole blue world And once
these children were the winds that moved my clouds.

Moonstruck

Like the good dog bitten

                by the good racoon bitten

                               by the good bat

                      that was just

            swooping up

          mosquitos

until the good bat

         was caught

                by the webby spore of virus:

                       rabies turns all of us bad

               traveling as it does on unreliable moonbeams, the pieces

of moon that break

          apart with sparks

              to fling themselves

                        earthward.

                She was moonstruck

        a daughter with an itch

that ached

        like chattering teeth

             to be scratched into bleeding

                   the way shame

             bleeds,

           crying *die, die*

       will you just

let me die?

        She tumble stumbles

               into what she doesn't want but also wants

                             so

                      badly

           that moon struck

        falling

daughter:
　　　　those candied embers and pillowy waters
　　　　　　　　　　　　are vertigo's sirens
　　　　　　　　　　　　　　　　　warning
　　　　　　　　　　against demons
　　　　　　or disease
　　　　that has breached

the labyrinth
　　　　　　of her body—of any
　　　　　　　　　　　　　　　body's
　　anti-
bodies—
　　　　where the minotaur ruminates
　　　　　　　　　　its vestibular fodder
　　　　　　　　　　　　from the manger
　in the black center

　　　　　of any child.

　　　　　　At the doorway
　　　　　　the ManGod lit
　　　　　　by auriscope
　　　　　　or prayer
　　　　　　carries blood
　　　　　　red hope.
You, her father, you name that ManGod.　　You, her mother, you name that hope.

Heaven

The therapist who warned me that I would be killed
by my husband (wrong, so far, so good) also said:
"Love thy neighbor as yourself assumes you love
yourself. So God expects you love yourself."

Hey, she said next. *Hey. Where'd you go?* To heaven,
I think, if heaven feels like a bolt fired by a crossbow
into that deepest part of me that I always forget is there.
Because even if love is what God feels like, it kills me
every time.

On a bad day, in heaven, I think, all of my clothes
will feel like cozy pajamas but smell of wood smoke.
In heaven, on a regular day, I hope for room enough
to stand behind the naturally good people—in the back,
I think, unless the rule is in play where the last is first
and the first is last rule, whereupon I hope instead
for room enough to stand near the front.

I admit some trepidation concerning the revelatory
creatures with all of the eyes and maybe some about
the bloodied martyrs as well who emerge from beneath
 the throne. At the same time, I would like to openly
support for having lived their faith to this extreme.

On earth, thirsty as dust and sand we sing:
there was no rain in the forecast; no dew in the morning;
no cloud on the horizon; no rain no rain no rain,
until it arrives in torrents. We will sing until heaven
is satisfied enough by our longing for heaven to make the air
thicken to hold us, to encase us, like heavy mud.

Below us will be the future, like decades of pain
we have hated to endure but that now inspires us
to twinkle: we are twinkling. Look at our angelic
twinkling selves: we are strangers, my beloved; we are
strangers and we are also cousins sharing a childhood.

Have mercy, brothers and sisters. Some of us
were never children. Some of us were never good.
Some of us were never virgins, wise or otherwise.

Turn me towards everything true. Open me to it.
Allow it to cut me. Bleed. Clot. Scar. Cut again.
All biological creatures suffer in their bodies—move me
beyond hurt into some other way of being. Until You
and I wrap around each other like long silken scarves
twisting upwards, always upwards, in a strong wind,
I pray that you make heaven on earth into the church
that welcomes all of us.

Harvesting the Traminette

September, a day
of sunshine and
puffy, sculptured
clouds. The puppies
chasing, chasing, then
dropping to pant. We
each had our own pair
of sharp clippers. We each
had our own white bucket
to collect the traminette
grapes we then dumped
into the wagon parked
at the end of the row.

The baby was with us, asleep
in his baby bucket
in the shade of the vines.
And we moved
slowly because the abundance
of the grapes was hidden
among the leaves.

The grapes! Pale green jade. Fat
full green bunches tumbling
into our hands, each grape
so taut with juice that some
of them burst upon touching
our skin. Burst then
dripped, then splashed
onto our skin and clothes
and hair. Little streams and
creeks and rivers of juice
so sweet, so sticky, that bees
counted us as flowers
and licked the sugar
right off of our hands.

The bees never stung.
The baby only cooed
and slept, cooed and slept.
The wagon was full
and then full again
and then full again.

We were family and that day
family meant working
together, sometimes working
so hard that we didn't want
to talk or laugh. At the end
of the day, we were glad
to be tired and sore and
sticky and the smell
of sweetness followed
us into our dreams.

The kingdom of God is like unto this.

On 70 East, Halfway Home

Columbus on the left rises up like Oz, so unreal
no one could ever live there. We ride across
an overpass into a horizon of heavy cloud,
enveloping, pervasive, like my human need
for my mother to always love me.

The speed limit is like running through water
in a dream. That slow. I pass every car, every semi
truck and camper. Having left my mother's
house, I want to be alone with my children
in my own home. In the backseat, my daughter
weeps for a return to her grandmother's lap,
her cats and her pie. Someday, her relief
in leaving me behind will be as inescapable
as her grief is now.

My mother, a nurse, shows her love
with nurse's corners so tight my feet bend
backwards beneath the sheet. The walls
of my childhood bedroom were painted a clean white,
representing her commitment to science
and reasons and pragmatic interpretations.
As a believer, my mother believes.
As a nurse, the idea of the blood of Jesus
sends her running for a HazMat kit.

But the blood of Jesus was my baptism.
And I want miracles to supercede physics
and biology. I want water to walk on.
I want lepers healed instantly
and broken hearts bound up and my tears
saved in a special jar. I want deliverances
from oppression and interventions of angels.
I want God to thunder on the mountain
within me, to cast that mountain into the sea
and to blaze without burning. I want to live

the belief that the homeless man on the corner
is an angel in disguise.

My mother and I have long since stopped
hinting for the other to be different. I can't sleep
with covers on my feet but I know
what she is trying to say by making up my bed.

Outside the Air Force Base

Molach roars, hungry
for our children, their heads
small and smooth, their hands
not always clean with the bulk
of newly taut muscle beneath
spackled green and brown
and grey and black uniforms
This time the name of the fire
is Kosovo. This time the name
of the fire is Iraq. Afghanistan.
Yemen. Who is it who requires
sacrifice of children so young
that they do not understand
what time means. They think
it means nothing. They think
it means a single tour—four years.
And then four more and longer
to live the unearthly visions.
Someone draws back
the string of a bow to shoot
stars across the blue sky.
What is life at the center
of the bull's eye? You live
with artificial thunder
and night vision goggles.
Look! There! in the sky!
Some foreign thing—arrowhead?
Squid claw? Gargoyle? Angel of Death?

Why the Body Needs the Body

The part of my lineage into the family of Jesus that I know
off hand travels from Sister Diana to Sister Caroline
to me to Anne, my former roommate, who witnessed my conversion—

it looked, she said, like I walked into a revolving door
and came back out a different person. A glowing person, still damp
from baptism. But then something made me a woman with an issue
of blood, made me a leper or the cynical thief resentful of his cross.

Anne said, out of a blue day, I'm going to pray you
the Bible back. Because the Bible had been used
to gouge out my deepest wounds. For years,
I had tried to walk without feet, tried to eat without hands
or a mouth. Could you pray me some cash
instead? I asked joking and not joking.
Because what I need is cash. And Anne,
whose provision was a soup line of miracles, who
never laughed.

about the things of God, laughed but didn't laugh. She did pray.
And then—poof!—there it was! The Word! *Fear not*, it sang to me
from the branches outside outside of my window, *Fear not, little flock!*

Arise, Talitha! jingling like dimes in my change jar. *He is able,*
rising with the steam from my milky sweet coffee cup, *to keep you
from falling! and to present you faultless before Him! with exceeding joy!*

The Word can be a mace, a flail or a battle ax or a kaleidoscope
of self reflection, a concave mirror into the heart of God. A sword
but not a weapon. Insight without accusation. From one mouth,
condemnation. From the mouth of my sister, life.

Think it not strange, the Bible explained as it set my bones
and sewed up my lacerations. *Such as is common to mankind.*

The principalities, the powers, the heights, the depths
His Love hops over like a curb on a city street;
the Lord of Glory cups my chin to speak the Word: *Daughter,*
daughter, you have sold yourself for nothing
but I have purchased you without money.

Fish

Teach a man to fish. Teach him to choose
the right bait for the right fish; teach him
to gauge the shadows of a lake, to remain
silent, to test the direction and force
of wind with a wet finger. Teach him
how to cast, how to tie a fly to look
like a fly, how ease the line or flip it, a little,
to make the bait twitch. How to hold
the fish down to pull out the hook,
how to gut the fish. What to do
with the head and the tail and the bones.

These are the useful and appropriate
lessons of self-reliance. But it's possible
that maybe his hands are old or cracked
or stiff. Maybe his thumb has been torn
from hauling and stacking bricks or from
the sharp tab of a beer can. It's possible
that all of his misery was driven by the engine
of his own mistakes. That he is grass mown
down by his own mower. But the meal is his,
if you teach him well, if he can fish, and if
he is also lucky. This is wisdom
that you can read from any number
of bumper stickers as you sit in traffic.

But what if . . . what if . . . what if . . . you
made the exception for no reason
and just gave him the fish instead?
What if you used your skill to catch
 and then clean and even steam a fish,
add some rice, a few vegetables you grew
with your own hands in your garden;
what if you stir the perfect sauce, creamy,
lemony, a sauce you labor over. What if
you twist a garnish—for no reason—

of orange slice and parsley, tucked to the side
of the entrée and what if you slide that plate—
make it the good china—in front of a man who
did not, could not, earn it—who might never
deserve it, who might even lack the capacity
to appreciate it? What if, as he takes his first bite,
sitting at the family table, the food is still hot?

So he rests from the work, for one meal.
And as he rests, maybe he remembers something
beautiful—his mother, maybe, and the child
he once was. A day full of sunlight or a day
that it finally, finally, finally rained. For the length
of one meal he remembers or does not not remember
and that night he will dream or not dream—whichever
is better for him—of the meal you made
with your own hands as he sleeps wherever men
who don't know how to fish tend to sleep.

What would this cost you? The money. True. The money.
The time. And it would cost you the knowledge
that you didn't teach one of life's hard lessons.
But you did teach yourself a different one—the one
where you learn that it is impossible
to claim wisdom without generosity.

Here he is, seated at your table, a man.
And here in your hand, a choice:
the fish or the hook?

Gray

Something about the way that we become gray.
How the first few strands or patches hide
in plain view until we see its shimmer in the mirror
unexpectedly. How long has that been there?
Age is the car traveling along, negotiating
with the speed limit. Time is the blur, whirling by
outside of the window. Time is something we think
we can pull out and disregard, shimmer by shimmer.

The darkest colors of our hair hides in back
where we can't easily see it but the lightest strands,
the silver and the white, walk with us into the sun:
we want so much to be our best selves, want so much
to be good and to be seen as good and to see ourselves
as good that it's easy to never hold a mirror to a mirror
in order to recognize and name our own darkness.

We age until our messy nests are abandoned
snarls of sticks and spit and string and feathers
and guano and our bird-bones are fragile and full
of fear. We molt loss and should have wishes.
We pray for wisdom but resist how much time
insists upon change. Our thoughts are garments
we probably should have probably outgrown.

Still, with light framing our faces, there to remind us that
repentance is the greatest act of faith—that the prodigal
could never have stopped in his path without believing
that home was waiting where it always waited—and that we
can realign our hearts in any kind of darkness and that someday

all of our mirrors will reflect the angelic transparency
that we have become. Light will shine from our center,
from our hearts of flesh and not stone, in all directions. And it will be
His light, not ours that shines. We will be the glass. We will be
the shimmer in the clean, silver mirror.

Thousands of People Tricked into Praying

(for a Dog with Ham on its Face)
Elements of this poem are modified from a Facebook posting by Stephen Roseman

This poor dog.

This poor dog
so badly burned
so horribly
disfigured
after he heroically
attempted to o
r actually did
save his family
from a house fire.

He might have been a rescue
dog now doing the rescuing.
He might have been set afire
by someone evil and broken
enough to do something like that.

The Facebook math goes like this:
One like = one prayer,
one share = ten prayers
for the dog to receive God's healing.
(Do not worry. We know you
don't actually "like" injured animals.)

Animal lovers around the world
who were also devout
in their relationship with their God
or gods fell to their knees
after seeing a dog with its entire face
so badly burned. His eyes. You couldn't
even see his eyes. His eyes were burned

away leaving a blindingly pink scab
across his gently sniffing dog face.
Thousands of people sent prayers
and love. "Prayers for this sweet dog,"
one Facebook user wrote.

The post has been shared
more than 100,000 times.
Which adds up to more
than a million prayers,
not counting the individual likes.

But the innocent creature suffers
nothing less than the searing
smell of ham so close to his nose.
A hoax about prayer: is nothing
sacred? And what about these
prayers rocketing about, unguided,
misguided, missiles?

We know so little about our own world.
Even less about the invisible world.
I am not ashamed to have prayed
any prayer—even prayers
where the answer clearly reveals
how stupid I am for love.

I do not care whether or not
my uninformed, misinformed prayers
live as smooth pebbles
that God skips across a sky shaped
lake or if my prayers are mixed into a stew
or sorted into specific bins
for specific reasons only with some
of them filed under miscellaneous
if even one prayer might bless
a vulnerable creature or minister
to heartaches I know nothing about.

And I am not ashamed when my people
are easily tricked—if they live heart first
and mind second, laying self-righteousness
aside to weep at even feigned cruelty.
I am not afraid to be the right kind of fool,
praying for people, not at people.
Help me help, O Lord. But not as a judge.

Still, the photo of the dog
blindfolded by lunchmeat
continues to be shared.
One like = one prayer,
one share = ten prayers.

Angels Trouble the Water

We are buoys, we are dolphins, we are seahorses, we are seals
and walruses, salmon and trout and flying fish some of us
squawking like gulls some of us crippled on land but some of us
dancers hiding the bulk of ourselves—icebergs!—beneath the light
blue water. We are mostly women, mostly old, mostly fat, buoyant
with our mother flubber; some of us
are pregnant snow globes or ripe avocados.
One young willowy girl with dark hair wears a bathing suit skirt
as if she is more ashamed of her body than the rest of us are of ours.

The two men regulars are Bill and the Other Guy. Bill is the old man
with bearskin hair on his chest, shoulders and back that moves in water
like sea grass, shifting as though it nurtures schools
of tiny fish. Bill is recovering from a stroke. The Other
Guy is hairless except for his forceful black eyebrows.
Minus the eyebrows, the Other Guy looks like a giant baby
as he flirts with the instructor even though he is married and
even though his wife bobs alongside of him, silent as a manatee
in the ebb and flow of his not funny jokes. Occasionally,
a young man with very dark skin slips in among us, never
looking at any of us; we have noticed
him not looking so we respectfully do not look at him
either—not directly. He swims laps after class while the rest of us
limp to the hot tub in order to stew like ingredients.

From six to seven pm, four days a week we do Aquafit at the same gym
where the crazy man, adrift on private tides, shot up
the salsa dancing class four years ago, killing three
women, one of them pregnant. Our pool water
is saline, not chlorine; the water is thicker than regular pool water,
more like tears. Gailya, our instructor, is tiny and mean.
Her arms are twining vines; she has hips like the banana seat
of a 1960's girl's bike. Gailya targets our core, our triceps
and our obliques. We march like tin soldiers, scuttle like crabs, run
in place, do jumping jacks, cross country ski. We jump
jump kick. We frog jump. We punch the water. We weave our arms

in figure 8s. We trot in a circle in one direction and then turn
to plunge against the current we have made ourselves. We kick the water
into frothy soup leaning back on our noodles. Frothy noodle soup.

The lifeguard is a boy who also distributes the water weights and noodles.
The lifeguard does his homework and taps on his phone while we swim.
He does not flinch at the sight of us lumbering up out of the water.
He has allowed none of us to drown.

I joined Aquafit after the boy in my freshman English class killed himself
with a gun as we entered the fourth act of Macbeth. Beneath the water
is far away from his empty desk but it is not always far
enough away and blood is everywhere I look or read.
Oh bleak bleak bleak cistern of tears. Grief seeps into everything,
everywhere, even here, under this water, this baptism of loss.
Lamentations, I cry, for all of the lost boys. Lamentations for the sword
that we choose to live by. He pleads from heaven, speaking from within
our collective stony hearts, calling for rethinking, repentance
and He hunkers down beside me
to share in my anguish and my suffering.

Redemption

like a coupon that arrives in the mail
printed on the back pages
of the Penny Saver, on newsprint
that smudges your hands black,
redemption slips into the house
with the least important mail.

      It rises up! From the heaps! From the compost
      heaps, from the composting barrels and heaps!
      Like dead leaves that have fallen from a tree
      and is raked into heaps!

            Redemption, excited, shouts its ordinary conversations
                    in a quiet room!

               and unfolds from the grasping fingers of the
                    rake and
               tumbles from the recyclable leaf bag that waits
               on the curb with the red-brown dead needles
               on a still twinkling Christmas tree next to a
                    stump
               of a tree with thick mealy rotted branches that
                    was
               knocked down by the storm—redemption

                      pulls me rising from the heaps
                      from the compost heaps and barrels
                      attaches me again to the stem to
                      the twig and to the branch now
                      greening away from the dark decay
                      and then fading to paler, paler green,
                      the sun becomes suddenly warm
                          enough
                      exactly, perfectly warm, with a gentle
                      spatter of rain, for roots to suckle

back into the breast of cultivated
ground.

Look! Look! I have produced
a seed!
Redemption! Anew! Again!

Poem for This Sunday

Already half a day gone, the kind of day
where one of the words we use is peace.
Again: peace. Peace like good food,
like sunlight filling valleys and canyons.
Somehow He provides us with something
solid, the heft of it like a smooth stone
in my hand. Something enveloping, like music
on the radio in the car on the way home from church.

This Sunday, we are waterlogged with peace,
as though we swam too long and played too long
in a pool or a lake or an ocean or as if we had
hiccupped too many times. So waterlogged,
we want naps. So waterlogged, we are unable
to feel our discontent.

This Sunday, what I want my children to remember:
how patient we were with each other on the way home
from church, how easily we laughed. How much peace
we had and at what cost.

How Much the Body

Begin with the nose, the smell of heat
from the sun on a field of grass. Salt water
and its tang of metal. Move to the ear
and the song of any song bird; to the eye
at the bounce of that bird alighting
on a thin branch. Above, watch the angelic
authority of the wingspan of an eagle. Dusk
purples the tree line on hills
in the distance and then morning eases
pink and orange into yellowy sunlight.
Then home comes into view. Then
the sensation of touch and a breeze
that winds across the back of the neck—a thread
of breeze, so slight, so cool. Against your hand,
the quick heart of a small animal. The softness
of its fur. The impulsive embrace of a human child.
Go back to the nose again, along with the heart,
to the powdery sweet scent of mother and the ear rejoices
at the occasion of her laughter. Laughter that bubbles
up. Tears that leak out. How much the body wants
what it was created to want. How much the body longs
to be alive—to share the meal and its smell of fresh bread and to taste
the sweetsour tang of new wine with beloved friends.

Remember me, He says.
Do this in remembrance of me.

www.ingramcontent.com/pod-product-compliance
Lightning Source LLC
LaVergne TN
LVHW051709080426
835511LV00017B/2809